D0564067

THE LIFE & TIMES OF

Adolf Hitler

BY
Ian Schott

This edition printed for, Shooting Star Press Inc, 230
Fifth Avenue, Suite 1212, New York, NY 10001

Shooting Star Press books are available at special discount
for bulk purchases for sales promotions, premiums, fund-
raising or educational use. Special editions or book
excerpts can also be created to specification. For details
contact – Special Sales Director, Shooting Star Press Inc.,
230 Fifth Avenue, Suite 1212, New York, NY 10001

This edition first published by Parragon Books
Produced by Magpie Books Ltd, 7 Kensington Church
Court, London W8 4SP
Copyright © Parragon Book Service Ltd 1994
Cover picture & illustrations courtesy of: Mary Evans
Picture Library.

ISBN 1 57335 046 X
A copy of the British Library Cataloguing in Publication
Data is available from the British Library.

Typeset by Hewer Text Composition Services, Edinburgh
Printed in Singapore by Printlink International Co.

FAILURES

Adolf Hitler was born on 20 April 1889 at Braunnau, Austria, then a part of the Austro-Hungarian Empire. His father, Alois, was a customs official. Adolf's mother, Klara, was Alois's second cousin and when she was sixteen she became his third wife.

Hitler was the fourth of five children, but only he and his half-witted sister Paula survived infancy. His half-sister, Angela Raubal, had a child, Geli Raubal, who was to be one of the loves of his life.

Alois was violent towards Klara and the children. He died when Adolf was fourteen, and Klara subsequently spoiled her son. He disappointed at school. Though not without promise, he was variously described as arrogant, argumentative, evasive, sly and lazy, with a leaning to melodrama. He reserved his enthusiasm for playing wargames and reading adventure stories about the North American Indians.

Young Adolf failed to gain a school leaving certificate, dropping out through illness. When he was sixteen he went to Linz, where he was to spend two years. He had decided his vocation was art and his intention was to enter the Vienna Academy of

Arts, but he repeatedly put off taking the entrance examination.

Instead, supported by his indulgent mother, he dallied in Linz, sketching, painting and drawing designs for the reconstruction of the city. He dressed like a rich student, and was thrilled when he was mistaken for the genuine article. Literature, architecture, music and painting all attracted him, though he persisted with none of them. To his dying day, Hitler was vexed by the thought of his unexploited gifts.

Music certainly had a profound influence on him, particularly the operas of Richard Wagner steeped in pessimistic romance and mythological themes, but lacking in humour. They later provided valuable inspiration for Hitler's own morbid philosophies and staged spectacles – he was to dictate *Mein Kamp* to the strains of Wagner playing on a wind-up gramophone. Hitler particularly cherished the gloom of *Parsifal*, which he saw more than thirty times.

In 1907, he finally took the entrance exam for Vienna, and failed. He was outraged and demanded to see the director, who fobbed him off, telling him he was probably better suited to architecture. Hitler took him at his word, and stayed on in Vienna to pursue his 'studies'. He apparently lied to his companions about his failure to pass the exam, and when they became curious as to why he never got out of bed, exploded into bitter rage at the philistines who had spurned him.

In Vienna, some maintain, Hitler contracted syphilis from a Jewish prostitute. It is claimed that Heinrich Himmler tried to persuade a Finnish doctor to attempt a cure for Hitler's syphilis in 1942; and a team of American military psychologists hypothesized that it was as a consequence of his formative experiences, which may have included syphilis, that Hitler required young women to urinate and defecate upon him.

At the time of Hitler's sojourn, Vienna had a large and prosperous Jewish population, and Jews dominated cultural life. Jealousy of their material or intellectual accomplishments was common. Anti-Semitic pamphlets were cheap and easy to read. Most of the ideas Hitler later claimed were his original product were in fact lifted from the scribblings of a defrocked priest, Lanz von Liebenfels, who blamed all ills on the defiling of 'pure' German blood by Jews. Such pamphlets lingered on the sexual aspect, which Hitler was to echo frequently: in *Mein Kampf* he evoked 'The nightmare vision of the seduction of hundred, of thousands of pure German girls by repulsive, crooked-legged Jew bastards.' The pamphlets were placed on his bookcase, next to his collections of pornography, mythology and the occult. It was Liebenfels who urged the mystic power of the swastika and the use of the 'ancient German runes' formed by the twin lightning flashes, later the insignia of the SS. To compound Hitler's isolation, his mother died of cancer. He was distraught.

Hitler tried again to get into the Vienna Academy of Arts, and this time was refused permission to take the examination. At the end of 1908 he left his lodgings, and vanished into the underbelly of Vienna.

Hitler claimed that during the following years he experienced hardship, poverty, unemployment; in short, real life. But in reality he still had a good supply of money from private sources, which he augmented by selling his sketches of Vienna. He later claimed that he had read voraciously, but he instead browsed the works of great authors, acquiring useful quotes which might be used to illustrate his world-philosophy.

'I read to confirm my ideas', he said. He was frightened of education, preferring the certainty of easy prejudice. He became a great source of imprecise, generalized knowledge, though he certainly knew the specification of every gun, tank and battleship on the market.

Vienna suffered from heavy unemployment, social injustice and left-wing unrest. It had a large population of immigrant workers and the poor lived badly. But there was little fervent nationalism to be found among the masses. Hitler, though born in Austria, now classed himself as a pure German, and was shocked by the lack of patriotism and the popularity of Communism. He saw this as the work of the Jews.

'In the face of that revelation, the scales fell from my eyes. My long inner struggle was at an end . . . Thus I finally discovered who were the evil spirits leading our people astray.'

Communism, the child of the Jewish economist and philosopher, Karl Marx, was naturally the personification of the Jewish conspiracy. It was also internationalist – it held that equality should transcend nationality, colour and race. In this it denied both the nationalism to which

Hitler was drawn, and his individual unique-
ness. He preferred Social Darwinism – the
'aristocratic principle of Nature' in which all
life was engaged in a struggle from which only
the fittest emerged alive.

In 1909, Hitler fell upon truly bad times. He
ended up on the streets, hungry and home-
less, surviving on hand-outs of soup and
living in a shelter for the destitute. From
1910 to 1913 he stayed in a charitable home
for men, where he monopolized the reading
room as a forum to lecture a captive audience. He scraped a living selling postcards of
vienna copied from photographs.

In 1913, Hitler moved to Munich, in the
Prussian heartland of Bavaria. He told friends
that he intended to enter the Munich Art
Academy. Though he did nothing about

this, he did fall in love with the city. 'A German city! So different from Vienna, that Babylon of races!'

He styled himself 'painter and writer' and lived an isolated existence, speaking to few apart from the family he lodged with, though he regularly had bitter quarrels in cafés. He had neglected to register for military service in Vienna, and was arrested in Munich. He pleaded for clemency, claiming to be ignorant of the law, and was excused both his misdemeanours and – after examination – military service on the grounds of 'physical weakness'.

In 1914, Germany and Austria declared war on Russia and Serbia. Internal differences and unrest were forgotten; national unity broke out, along with an ecstatic sense of patriotism. The German Kaiser declared everyone to be 'German brothers', and to millions war brought an end to everyday monotony and a simple direction in life – to fight. Hitler was enthusiastic.

'For me these hours came as a deliverance . . . I sank down on my knees to thank Heaven for the favour of having been permitted 'to live in such a time.'

He volunteered for the army, and to his delight was accepted. After training he was sent to the front, where he was a regimental runner from 1914 to 1918. The position suited him; he could barely be persuaded to take leave. It was lonely and dangerous work. He remained aloof from his fellow soldiers who quickly lost their enthusiasm for the war, for which he accused them of treachery.

Adolf Hitler

Hitler with Göring at a rally

Without exception, his comrades found him dreary. He was decorated with the Iron Cross but not promoted beyond corporal. He appeared to relish the horrors of the trenches and regarded an indifference to suffering as proof of manhood. 'War', he was fond of saying, 'is for a man what childbirth is for a woman.'

Hitler was lying in hospital, suffering from the after-effect of a gas attack, when news came of the Armistice. By the Treaty of Versailles, Germany was required to make vast payments to its former enemies in compensation. In addition, 13 per cent of its territory was taken away, and it was disarmed. For Hitler, and other nationalists, it was a moment of complete humiliation, and they never forgave those who signed the treaty.

RISE TO POWER

After the war German society was deeply divided. Communism gained ground, and not only among the poorest of the country, but among liberals and intellectuals. The right wing, with which many disaffected soldiers aligned themselves, also had wide support. Intellectual notions of German *volk* and *kultur* were popular. *Volk* translates as 'people', but, as with many words favoured by the Nazis, it appeals beyond that, to a sense of shared racial identity in a racial homeland. Hitler was fond of using '*volk*' and '*volkisch*', and held that, while other nations had bourgeois civilization, the Germans had '*kultur*', which indicated passion beyond reason. As Hitler put it:

'. . . we must be ruthless . . . we are barbarians! We want to be barbarians! It is an honourable title!'

Hitler, failed school-pupil, failed artist, and social misfit, first went to a meeting of the German Workers' Party on 12 September 1919. He was still in the military, working for the Munich District Command, writing reports on right-wing political parties. The army actively encouraged those groups it thought useful to the cause. In the course of his 'work', Hitler produced a report for his commanding officer on 'the danger Jewry constitutes to our people today', in which he wrote:

'The anti-Semitism of reason . . . must lead to the planned legal opposition to and elimination of the privileges of the Jews. Its ultimate goal, however, must absolutely be the removal of the Jews altogether.'

His sentiments were quite clear, and never changed.

He was disappointed with the Workers' Party at his first encounter, but went again with the encouragement of the founder, who had been impressed by Hitler's fluency in a tirade he had launched at his first meeting. Hitler, after some hesitation, joined the Party as the member responsible for recruitment and propaganda. On 16

October 1919 he made his first public speech.

Indeed, he proved an animated, passionate speech-maker, with the ability to appeal to the emotions of his audience and to feed off their fears and hopes. He soon had the name of the party changed to the 'National Socialist German Workers' Party' – the Nazis – and by 1921 had become its Führer.

He planned a party that would have the widest possible social appeal by having no specific policies. Instead, the Nazis attacked the 'causes' of Germany's downfall – foreigners and Communists in general, Jews in particular – whilst asserting that Germany might be great again. There was no television, and restricted access to radio, so spoken and written propaganda were vital. Hitler's skill as a performer was used to best advantage at the huge, staged rallies of the 1930s, when there was a peculiarly sexual relationship between him and his audiences.

'The psyche of the broad masses is like a woman' observed Hitler, 'subject to a vague emotional longing for the strength that completes her being, and who would rather bow to a strong man than a weakling. . . . Liberal teaching offers them a choice. They have no idea how to make such a choice and are prone to feel they have been abandoned . . .'

When his performance was united with the vast stage spectacles of the Nuremberg rallies, the effect was overwhelming. In spite of his passion, he never lost sight of his objectives in a speech; the whole experience remained calculated. He would practise his facial expressions in the mirror for hours, and take a long time to warm up, to sense the mood of his audience, before moving into gear with a series of simple, repeated statements and questions to which the audience could only answer 'yes' or 'no'. A speech lasted around two hours, and he always left his audience with an optimistic ending, wanting more. In the crucial elections of the 1930s, he would make several speeches a night, dashing around the country by aeroplane.

As Otto Strasser, one of the original Nazis who later deserted Hitler, said:

'Hitler responds to the vibrations of the human heart with the delicacy of a seismograph . . . or perhaps of a wireless set . . . enabling him to act as a loudspeaker proclaiming the most secret desires, the least admissible instincts, the suffering and personal grievances of a whole nation . . . He sniffs the air . . . he gropes . . . he feels his way . . . senses the atmosphere. Suddenly he bursts forth. His words go like an arrow to their target . . . telling it what it most wants to hear . . .'

He was bolstered by propaganda in the form of newspapers and pamphlets, and pseudo-religious, mystic symbolism with uniforms, swastikas and titles. Hitler took personal charge of choosing all this. Later, Joseph Goebbels was the Nazi Minister for Propaganda. Hitler was quick to see the propaganda use of technology. His use of aeroplanes, for example, in an age when they were still regarded with a certain superstitious amazement, helped to enhance his

The Reichstag is burnt down

Hitler with 'Brownshirts'

image as an omnipresent Messiah descending from the skies.

Propaganda was backed up with violence. The Nazis formed a paramilitary wing called the SA, or 'Brownshirts'. These thugs, made up of disillusioned ex-soldiers, carried out whatever intimidation and brutality was necessary against political rivals, particularly the Communists. The head of the SA was Ernst Rohm, a corpulent ex-soldier, who had a team of pimps scouring the school-yards of Munich to keep him supplied with the boys that were his pleasure. Hitler's company was generally unsavoury; a collection of misfits, hunchbacks, sexual bandits, seedy ex-convicts, decadent aristocrats and occultists.

The Kaiser had been forced to abdicate, and Germany had highly unstable governments, cobbled together from endlessly quarrelling coalitions of parties, which toppled monthly. Depression and inflation added to the chaos. In November 1923, a thousand billion marks had the spending power that one solitary mark had had in 1914. Germany had to pay crippling compensation to her former enemies. In Italy the Fascists were in the ascendant, and Hitler's new party was successful enough for him to attempt a violent take-over of the State of Bavaria in November 1923.

Starting with a meeting at a beer cellar in Munich, the Nazis planned to march eventually on Berlin itself. Hitler was uneasy about the whole event, but was persuaded that there would be support from the army and police. The plan was a fiasco, and Hitler was distinguished by his lack of heroism. The

Bavarian Police opened fire, killing sixteen, and Hitler was imprisoned. Though sentenced to five years, he served only nine months. During this time he wrote *Mein Kampf* with its 164,000 grammatical and syntactical mistakes, enjoyed considerable comfort and received as many visitors as he pleased.

On his release he was fêted. His company was sought at the houses of the rich and famous, he dined with industrialists, and spent weekends at the home of Winifred Wagner, granddaughter of his idol.

Hitler enjoyed great support among the wealthy of Germany, who feared the spread of Communism. Many sources of Nazi funding remain a mystery, but they did receive support from industrialists and

tycoons like the newspaper magnate Alfred
Hugenberg. Hitler also charmed cash out of
old ladies, and some money came from
America. None the less, when success
came the Party was on the verge of bank-
ruptcy.

Throughout the 1930s Hitler enjoyed Mer-
cedes limousines, apartments in Munich and
a new-found popularity with women. But,
of the seven women thought to have had
relationships of some sort with Hitler, six
committed or attempted to commit suicide.
One of these was Renate Mueller, a well-
known film actress, whom Hitler invited
back to his quarters one evening. She con-
fided to a director that Hitler had fallen to his
knees in front of her and begged to be
beaten. Shortly after relating this, she fell
out of the window of a Berlin hotel. This

was in 1937, with the Nazis in power; her death was ruled a suicide.

There was also Geli Raubal, daughter of his half-sister, Angela. On his release from prison, Hitler had summoned Angela and her daughter to work as his housekeepers. Geli was then aged seventeen and something of a beauty. Hitler established her in a Munich apartment, and paid for singing lessons. Hitler's infatuation was noted by his fellow Nazis, who complained that Hitler was 'excessively diverted from his political duties by the constant company of his niece'.

In 1929 Hitler exiled Geli's mother to his weekend house, and moved Geli in with him. They had separate bedrooms, but on the same floor. Geli was increasingly oppressed by Hitler's jealous attentions, and had been plotting to escape, when, on 18 September 1931, she apparently shot herself in the chest after an argument with 'Uncle Alf'. News of her death was suppressed and her body hastily buried with the co-operation of the Munich authorities.

Fritz Gerlich, a journalist who claimed to have conclusive evidence that she was murdered, was himself killed before he could print it; all his documents were burned.

Hitler was simultaneously having an affair with a schoolteacher's daughter, Eva Braun, which continued until their mutual suicide in 1945. He showed her little or no affection, never told her his whereabouts and flirted incessantly with other women, who found him charming despite his flabby

English translation of *Mein Kampf*

Jewish shops are attacked by Nazis

physique, spindly limbs and rotting teeth. He liked women who were petite and blonde.

Braun attempted suicide in 1932, and Hitler was more considerate thereafter.

Having failed to seize power by force, he was determined that he should triumph legally. He drove the Nazi Party on over ten years and countless disappointments. By 1932 it was the largest single party, with over 14 million votes, but it could not win an outright majority over the ruling conservative and nationalist coalition. Hitler forced election after election to destabilize the authorities, until they were at last compelled to do a deal with him and invite him to join the coalition.

Against a background of growing racial violence engineered by the Brownshirts, Hitler broke into the government in 1933 and took the position of Chancellor. The parties who had done deals with the Nazis in order to keep a measure of power had wrongly assumed that Hitler would simply prove a useful weapon against the Communists. Von Papen, the Vice-Chancellor, had boasted that Hitler was not to be taken seriously. The British firmly believed that the Nazis had peaked and no longer presented a threat.

27 February 1933, there was a fire, probably stage-managed, at the seat of Government, the Reichstag. It allowed Hitler to declare a state of emergency. On 23 March, under threat of using his legal powers to dissolve the government and throw the country in

chaos once more, he obtained an Enabling Act which gave him dictatorial powers and banned all other political parties.

PREPARING FOR WAR

Organizations and businesses were brought under Nazi control. Unions were banned and replaced with compulsory membership of Nazi Workers' parties. Schools began to teach a strictly nationalist syllabus. Nazi youth organizations sprang up. Membership of these became compulsory. By 1938 there were 7 million members of the Hitler Youth, and the remaining 4 million who had avoided it were ordered to join immediately. Hitler's attentions even extended to 'decadent' art. 7,000 paintings were removed from public view. Hitler ordered the burnign of books he considered corrupting.

Nazi intentions were simple. Faced with a country in a severe economic crisis, they tore up the Treaty of Versailles. They refused to pay compensation; they rearmed; they laid claim to Germany's lost lands and intended to further extend these to provide *Lebensraum*, or living room, for the German race; and they would solve the Jewish problem, which included the Communists. There were no plans for peaceful coexistence, only conquest.

Hitler took little interest in the day to day affairs of the Nazi state, and his henchmen quarrelled over power. His accomplices included Joseph Goebbels, the Minister for

Propaganda. He and his wife committed suicide in the bunker, having first given lethal injections to their six children. Goering, the Reich Marshal for Air, was fat, ruthless and popular, and addicted to luxury and drugs. Condemned to be hanged after the war, he poisoned himself. The man in charge of the Final Solution was Heinrich Himmler, who brought to the job his experience as a failed poultry farmer. He also ran the SS, the state within the state, which interfered with all other aspects of government. Bespectacled and nondescript, he committed suicide after being captured by the Allies.

Whilst preparing the nation for war, Hitler began to suffer physical illness. He had long been principally vegetarian because of bowel problems – abdominal pains, constipation and flatulence. He began to see a quack doctor, Theo Morrel, who became his constant companion. By the end of the war, Hitler was taking up to thirty drugs and vitamin compounds for his real and imagined complaints.

Driven by a policy of huge deficit spending, Germany rearmed and built the autobahns that would carry its troops to war. Germans marched in uniform, singing the hymns of Nazism. Families worshipped in the official church of the Nazi Party, the *Reichskirche*. They smashed the windows of Jewish shops; and they beat up Jews, and raped and murdered them with impunity. The first labour and death camps were established. By 1938, Germany faced a financial crisis, and Hitler could wait no longer to begin his war.

WAR

First to go was Austria, which was annexed as part of Germany without a fight. The Rhineland, under French occupation since the end of the Great War, had already been infiltrated by Hitler's soldiers. Czechoslovakia was attacked under the pretext of protecting a German minority. Neville Chamberlain, the British Prime Minister, flew to meet Hitler, and came back clutching a worthless agreement to 'peace in our time'.

Hitler regarded a war with the Soviet Union as inevitable. His racist theories ruled out coexistence with the Slavs.

'This Russian desert,' he later said, 'we shall populate it. We'll take away its character or an Asiatic steppe, we'll Europeanize it. With this object in mind we have undertaken the construction of roads. Studded along their whole length will be German towns and around these towns our colonists will settle . . .'

But he was concerned that Germany should not enter a war in the east until it was prepared militarily; to achieve this, Germany required raw materials from the Soviet Union. To this end, he engaged in prolonged diplomacy with Stalin.

His other hope was to keep Britain out of a European conflict, believing that the nation would see that its long-term interests lay in allying with Germany against the Communists.

In the event of war, Britain would look to support from the Soviet Union. By concluding a pact with Stalin – which he intended to renege on – Hitler hoped to convince Britain that it was useless to fight.

Stalin recognized that a war with an ascendant Germany was probable. But his military forces were depleted by the bloody purges of the 1930s. The army was ill equipped, demoralized and badly led – 50,000 of the officer corps had been destroyed. Stalin was therefore determined to acquire a belt of defensive territory running from Finland to

A parade of the Hitlerjugend

Hitler's home at Berchtesgaden

the Black Sea (he was to make eastern Poland the centre-piece), and to buy time. The poor state of the Red Army was emphasized by the invasion of Finland, begun on 30 November 1938. Stalin had compelled the Baltic States to accept garrisons of Russian troops, but Finland refused his demand to move their border away from Leningrad and lease him the port of Hanko. In the ensuing winter war, the Soviet troops were outfought by the Finns under the formidable Marshal Mannerheim, and Soviet losses were immense. Only in February 1939, after prolonged bombardment and an attack by 140,000 troops, did Stalin prevail. Offers of help from the British and French came too late. This poor showing by the Red Army convinced Hitler that an early attack on Russia could not fail.

Poland was Hitler's next strategic considera-
tion. Control of the country offered both a
traditional channel for an attack on the east
and, if he waged war in the west, a defensive
buffer against an attack from the rear.

Hitler planned to attack Poland on 26
August 1939. Throughout the summer he
battled to isolate Poland diplomatically, and
calculated that news of a Nazi–Soviet pact
would deter Allied intervention.

It was crucial that this pact should be
signed before the invasion. Stalin was
cautious; he was interested only in what
Russia might gain territorially, and to this
end a secret protocol was part of the
arrangement. In this, Germany agreed
that, in the event of the 'political transfor-
mation of eastern Europe', Poland would

be divided into German and Soviet spheres of interest, and Stalin would have control of the Baltic States. In late August, under pressure to force the signing, Hitler was compelled to write to Stalin personally. When he received Stalin's favourable reply, he exclaimed, 'I have them! I have them!' The attack had to be delayed for five days, but on 31 August the Germans launched a blitzkrieg which swept away the million-strong but antiquated Polish Army within hours.

Within twenty-one months of the Nazi-Soviet partition of Poland, approximately 2 million civilians had died. The SS murdered the population in the western sector; in the east, the Red Army pillaged the country and mounted a round of pogroms.

Britain and France declared war. There was no way back. 'I go the way that providence guides me' Hitler asserted, 'with the assurance of a sleep-walker.'

In April 1940, Hitler heard that the British were considering backing Norway's neutrality and landing troops there to cut the Sweden-Germany convoys of iron ore, deny Germany's U-boats the use of Norway's coastline, and create a springboard to send help to the Finns. The Germans landed first, and, though Hitler was nearly hysterical with anxiety during the fighting, by the end of May 1940 the British and French Forces in Norway were evacuated. Neville Chamberlain's government fell. On 10 May 1940, Winston Churchill, whom Hitler both hated and feared, became Prime Minister.

Poster for the 1936 Olympic Games

Hitler relaxing in the country

On the same day, after twenty-nine post-ponements, the attack in the west was launched. German forces smashed through the wooded countryside of the Ardennes, outflanking the Allied armies – a daring and completely successful plan devised by General Erich von Marsten. The Germans advanced so rapidly that Hitler lost his nerve several times, afraid that his tanks were too far ahead of the rest of his army. Though the opposing troops were numerically matched, the German tanks and aircraft were vastly superior and were used in highly effective combinations that the Allies did not know how to combat. Within six weeks, they had the French Army in tatters and the British on the beach at Dunkirk. It was here that Hitler decided to halt the advance, frightened by his success. Goering promised that the air force, the *Luftwaffe*, would finish off the British

troops. They failed, and the British managed the remarkable evacuation. On 10 June
Hitler finally persuaded the apprehensive
Mussolini to declare war; the Italians made
an undistinguished contribution to the
French campaign, but their presence was
not really necessary. On 22 June the French
signed an armistice; the Germans had taken
France at a cost of only 27,000 men.

With Europe in turmoil, Stalin completed
his annexation of the Baltic Republics in
the summer of 1940. On 2 August 1940
they were incorporated into the Soviet
Union.

On 27 July 1940 Hitler concluded the
Tripartite Agreement with Japan and Italy.
In September, after the abdication of King
Carol, Germany turned Romania into a

satellite under General Antonescu, securing its oilfields.

Hitler was now sure of his military genius, took less advice and shouted more. His quarrelling generals simply agreed with him. The planned invasion of England was to be preceded by massive air-strikes against military and civilian targets. On 'Eagle Day', 13 August 1940, Goering's air force began to bomb Britain. By 17 September, the raids had stopped in the face of huge losses. On one day, seventy-one aircraft were downed. Hitler could not afford to sustain these losses indefinitely. Britain's continued resistance forced Hitler to consider strategies in the Middle East, the Mediterranean and the Soviet Union.

Mussolini was jealous of Hitler's success. To regain some pride for Italy, he occupied

Greece in October 1940. Hitler was beside himself. His strategy had been that Italy should drive the British out of Egypt – in which they had failed – not create tensions elsewhere. Moreover, the Italians performed lamentably in Greece, and Hitler was obliged to divert forces to support them. Having failed to defeat Britain, German forces were now more extended than he had intended, and, though their military strength was unquestionable, they lacked the resources to continually expand; besides Germany's shortages of oil, steel and coal, it was to be two and a half years before the German economy was fully integrated into the war effort.

In November 1940, Ribbentrop, acting for Hitler, sought to seduce the Soviet Union still further, and distract them from their

European interests by bringing them into the Tripartite Agreement. The meeting with Stalin's envoy, Molotov, was conducted in an air-raid shelter. Ribbentrop urged the Soviets to join in the dismemberment of the British Empire. Britain, he insisted, was finished. The dour Russian listened carefully, and then said: 'If that is so, why are we in this shelter, and whose are these bombs that are falling?'

When Hitler realized that Stalin could not be distracted from Europe, he lost interest in negotiations and determined on a pre-emptive attack, though he was counselled continually that this would best be left until 1944. On 18 December 1940, he issued Directive No. 21 Operation Barbarossa, the invasion of the Soviet Union.

The Final Solution began in 1941. Poland was turned into an abattoir. Of the 18 million victims of Nazi brutality in Europe, 11 million died on Polish soil. Of that 11 million, 5 million were Jews. The names of the camps, in which, without compassion, young and old of both sexes were systematically gassed, shot, tortured, starved and worked to death are Dachau, Buchenwald, Belzec, Chelmno, Treblinka, Mauthausen and Auschwitz – the model for hell-on-earth, the heart of the Third Reich, and the summit of Hitler's art. It is still hard to comprehend how human beings who were not without emotion in other aspects of their lives could carry out such work without question, and find in it trial of their manhood. The programme proceeded with great secrecy until the end of the war. It was, said Heinrich

German troops march into Czechoslovakia

Hitler at the beginning of the War

Himmler, addressing the SS: '. . . a glorious page in our history that has never been and can never be written.'

Hitler was distracted from the invasion of the Soviet Union by Mussolini's failure in Greece, and by Yugoslavia, where army officers had rebelled against the regime's affiliation to the Nazis. He assigned seven Panzer divisions and 1,000 aircraft to attack the latter, and it was forced to capitulate after the *Luftwaffe* had bombed Belgrade for three days, killing 17,000 civilians. Later, though, the ferocious Yugoslav partisans under Marshal Tito would prove a crucial drain on German resources. Greece was occupied by the end of April 1941, and on 20 May Crete fell to a spectacular airborne operation. In North Africa, Rommel reversed the British victories over the Italians. Not for the last time, the professionalism of the German military had saved Hitler. This was his high point.

INVASION AND RETREAT

Hitler's great ally, both at that time and in the ensuing months, was Stalin. Stalin was surprised by Hitler's successes in the Balkans. But, far from anticipating that Hitler would turn on him, he signed a neutrality pact with the Japanese, maintained supplies to Germany, and reaffirmed Russia's friendly intentions.

Throughout the spring of 1941 the inscrutable Soviet leader was repeatedly warned by

American, British and by his own intelligence forces of an impending German attack. By late May, Marshal Zhukov could even identify the German units to be used, and their objectives. But Stalin ignored their warnings, and did not even show his generals the data he had received about German plans. He dismissed anything that did not fit in with his view of the situation as German propaganda, or British propaganda intended to force Russia into a war. He ordered his air force to allow the *Luftwaffe* to fly reconnaissance missions into Soviet territory without hindrance; it was as a consequence of this that most of the Soviet air force was later destroyed on the ground. Mobilization of the Red Army was ruled out.

In June, the British, who had cracked the

German code, notified Stalin of the precise
details of the German build-up. But he
responded by issuing a public statement
which decried the attempts of Britain to
destabilize Soviet-German relations. On 21
June, the evening before the attack, Hitler,
who had been suffering terribly from nerves,
drafted a proclamation which put all the
blame for the ensuing catastrophe firmly
on the Soviet Union. Then, immensely
cheered (as he always was when finally
embarked for action), he perked up, chose
a fanfare for his radio announcement, and
went to bed. On the Soviet side, Zhukov
knew that the Germans must attack the next
day, but was denied permission to mobilize,
on the grounds that this would provoke. No
Soviet units had instructions as to orders in
the event of hostilities. By the time Stalin
unwillingly agreed to the issuing of war

directives, the Germans had cut most communications, and the front-line Soviet units had no idea what was happening.

In the early hours of 22 June, bombing attacks were launched on Sevastopol, Minsk, Kiev and the Baltic States. Stalin's generals tried to contact him, but were told he was asleep, and could not be disturbed. At 3.30 in the morning, Zhukov, who had Stalin's private telephone number, managed to get through to him; his news was greeted with disbelief. The Politburo finally met at 4.30. Stalin was pale and sick.

Operation Barbarossa was in full swing. Three German Armies, comprising 3.2 million men, and thirteen motorized divisions, including 3,350 tanks, supported by troops from Finland, Romania, Slovakia and Hun-

13·MÄRZ 1938
EIN VOLK EIN REICH
EIN FÜHRER

Poster proclaiming a 'greater' Germany

German Stuka planes in action

gary, were carving up the Soviet Union. Army Group North made for the Baltic States and Leningrad; Army Group Centre headed direct for Moscow; and Army Group South was to take the Ukraine, overrun the industrial areas of the Dnieper, and take the Crimea and the precious oil reserves of the Caucasus.

Behind the orthodox troops went the *Einsatzgruppen*, the extermination squads sent to liquidate the 'Jewish-Bolshevik ruling class'. More than 300,000 civilians were killed in the first sixth months. Of the 5.7 million Russian prisoners taken, barely one million survived the war. The Germans had a genuine opportunity to exploit opposition to Stalin's regime and turn the Ukraine into an ally. But the policy of racist genocide prevailed, and all those

they overran were motivated to fight
tooth and nail.

The Germans could not afford a prolonged
campaign in the east. Hitler had argued that
the Soviet leadership would quickly collapse;
the British had estimated that Soviet resistance to the Germans might be expected to
last five or six weeks; in war-games, the
Soviet generals, taking the German part,
had thrashed themselves. At first the Germans made great progress. The Soviet forces
were poorly led and badly equipped, and
Stalin himself suffered something of a ner-
vous breakdown, retreating to his dacha.

But, within weeks, German progress slowed
as resistance units, though cut off and dis-
organized, continued to fight furiously.
Stalin recovered his nerve, reorganized his

high command, rehabilitated crucial officers he had imprisoned and, though his arrogance caused him to make dreadful tactical mistakes, he increasingly took good advice, particularly from the great Marshal Zhukov, who saved him from disaster on many occasions. The Soviet Union also managed to relocate vital industries in Siberia, and went on to produce equipment to match that of the Germans – the T34 tank and the Yak fighter aircraft.

Hitler's generals were in favour of a mighty thrust at the centre of the Russian front to destroy the bulk of the Soviet armour, but Hitler maintained war on three fronts. As a consequence, Army Group North became deadlocked at Leningrad – a siege that was to last 900 days. In the south, the Germans progressed better; but Operation Typhoon, the main thrust at Moscow, to which 800,000 men were committed, did not take place until late in the year, by which time fatigue and the weather had taken their toll of both troops and equipment. The battle for Moscow opened on 15 November, and by 5 December, as temperatures plummeted to $-40°$, the Germans had struggled to the outskirts of the city. There they were fought to a standstill, and the Soviet command then released its strategic reserve of 700,000 troops in a decisive counter-attack which brought about a loss of confidence among the German generals. Hitler refused to allow them to retreat; they dug in and stabilized the eastern front. But German forces were now spread out in a line from the Baltic to the Black Sea. They had lost their momentum, and the wisest realized that they could not prevail in a war of attrition. They had already suffered 750,000 casualties.

Italian newspaper report on Hitler's visit to Mussolini

Auschwitz prisoners after liberation

In May 1942, misconceived Soviet plans to liberate the Crimea and raise the siege of Leningrad resulted in catastrophic defeats. In June, Sevastopol fell and its army was destroyed by the Germans. Stalled in the north and centre, the German's summer attack – Operation Blue – had been to direct the bulk of Army Group South at the vital communications centre of Stalingrad. But with such good news elsewhere, Hitler was convinced that the Soviets were all but finished, and directed his forces to divide to take Rostov as well and move on the Caucasus oil-wells. The attack on Stalingrad was ultimately left to Paulus's Sixth Army, supplemented by assorted Romanians, Italians and Hungarians of dubious worth. Aided by the *Luftwaffe*, the Germans reached the northern suburbs of Stalingrad on 23 August. Stalin refused to allow any retreat from Stalingrad, and, led by Marshal Chuikov, Soviet resistance stiffened; by the time German reinforcements arrived, their forces were embroiled in the most savage battle of the war. Amid street-fighting, and hand-to-hand combat fought in doorways, stairwells and basements, the city was reduced to a desolate ruin. But the Red Army successfully disrupted organized German manoeuvres, and on 13 September an all-out German attack to divide Soviet forces and drive through to the Volga failed. In late November Soviet forces completed a massive encirclement of the Germans and on 31 January Paulus and his staff surrendered, defying Hitler's orders to fight to the death; Hitler insisted that Paulus should have shot himself.

The Red Army took more than 90,000 prisoners. The battle was the first major loss suffered by the Germans in Europe; the Red Army gained in confidence, and the Germans sensed defeat.

The news was particularly bad for Hitler. At the beginning of November it had become clear that he had lost the Battle of El Alamein, in North Africa, where the Afrika Corps and its Italian comrades had been driven back by numerically superior British forces. The British Eighth Army then set about chasing the Germans for 1,500 miles, until they had expelled them from North Africa altogether. America had joined the war, and the Allied bomber offensive on German cities and industrial centres had begun.

In the spring of 1943 the Germans straightened out their front line and made some gains, recapturing Kharkov. A major operation, Citadel, was planned for early summer. This would aim to encircle the concentration of Russian forces in the Kursk salient, between Moscow and the Sea of Azov, and drive through to Moscow again. But suspicions that the Allies were to attempt a landing in Italy caused the plan to be delayed until July. In the event, the Allies did invade Sicily. The delay allowed the Soviet Union to build up a massive concentration of forces in the salient; in April, there had been 1,200 Red Army tanks there, but by July this had swelled to more than 3,000.

Citadel was launched on 5 July. At the front of the German pincer movement were twenty Panzer divisions, including Hitler's pet Waffen SS units: SS Death's Head, SS Adolf Hitler and SS Das Reich. Little mercy was shown by either side. The Red Army was well dug in, and played to a plan, attriting the German forces until launching a counter-attack on 18 July. An extraordinary tank-battle erupted around Prokharovka, involving 1,000 vehicles. There were dreadful losses on both sides, but at the conclusion the Germans had exhausted their supplies of men and armour, and were on the verge of their long retreat to Berlin. They fought throughout with great tenacity. But by January Leningrad had been relieved, and in April German forces in the Caucasus were routed. The Allies were progressing through Italy, and Roosevelt, Churchill and Stalin were already planning the dismemberment of Germany; they called for its unconditional surrender.

DEFEAT

In 1944 Hitler began increasingly to isolate himself, rarely emerging from his rural hide-out, the 'Wolf's Lair', a depressing complex in the midst of a thick and gloomy forest in Prussia. He refused to read reports about the military situation. He ate with his secretaries who were forbidden to mention the war. After 1943, he made only two speeches.

Rather than sue for peace or seek practical ways to increase Germany's military hopes,

Hitler looked to miracle weapons. But his impatience ensured that he gave little serious attention to the atomic bomb. He invested Germany's resources in V1 and V2 rockets. These killed nearly 10,000 civilians, but they were militarily insignificant.

On 4 June the Allies occupied Rome. Two days later they landed in France. Rommel, who was in charge of coastal defences, was on his way to see Hitler when the news broke. Hitler was asleep, and no one dared disturb him. By the time he woke up in the afternoon and ordered that 'the enemy must be annihilated at the bridgehead by the evening of 6 June', the Allies were well ensconced. Within ten days, 600,000 troops were ashore; by the end of a month, nearly a million. Hitler could not accept it. He was convinced that the Allies could not hold together, that their alliance would collapse, that the British would fight the Russians, that his miracle weapons would destroy their spirit. In the east, the Russians advanced 300 miles in six weeks and expelled the Germans from their territory. They were only 400 miles from Berlin.

Some within the German military had always opposed the Nazis; others now realized the suicide that Hitler intended for Germany. Henning von Tresckow, one of a small number of high-ranking Army officers who were involved in the plot to kill Hitler that summer, wrote to his fellow conspirator, Klaus von Stauffenberg:

'. . . The assassination must be attempted at all costs . . . Even should it fail . . . we must prove to the world and to future generations that the men of the German Resistance dared to take this step and hazard their lives upon it . . .'

There had been various aborted attempts to kill the Führer, but finally, on 20 August, von Stauffenberg, crippled and blind in one eye with war-wounds, planted a brief-case with a bomb in it under a table in a conference room. After Hitler's death, the conspirators planned to use the Army to take Berlin and sweep the Nazis away. The bomb did explode, but Hitler survived.

In the resulting purge, the principal conspirators, who had gathered together in expectation of Hitler's death, were shot or committed suicide. Field Marshal von Witzleben, Generals Hoepner, von Hase and Stieff, together with four others, were hanged by piano wires from meat-hooks. The men, who had been tortured for days, showed considerable dignity. Another 200 civilians and military officers were executed. A further 5,000 were sent to concentration camps. Henning von Tresckow committed suicide by blowing his head off with a hand-grenade.

The failure of the plot rejuvenated Hitler's hopes. He was convinced Heaven had spared him, and that the defeats he had suffered were due to treachery on the part of his generals. For the little that remained of his life, he excluded anyone he did not feel was personally loyal to him. Goebbels, Himmler and Bormann, all Nazis, wielded the power. Each strove to establish a personal empire amidst the ruins.

On 25 August, Paris was liberated. On 11 September an American patrol crossed the German frontier. The war had come home to Hitler. 'In future, anyone who tells anyone else that the war is lost will be treated as a traitor', shouted Hitler, 'with all the consequences for him and his family.'

In December the Germans launched a desperate bid to break the Allied lines in the Ardennes with the object of taking Antwerp. The offensive was opposed by most of the surviving army officers. After initial successes, the Germans simply ran out of petrol at the Battle of the Bulge. They lost 100,000 men, 600 tanks, 1,600 aircraft and were compelled to withdraw. A month after the attack, they were once again in full retreat.

Hitler sought consolation in a vast, illuminated model of the rebuilding he planned for his home town of Linz. He was returning in his mind to those far-off days when, posing as a student, he had sketched and dreamed of the great destiny that lay in store for him.

His mind roamed over the causes of Germany's predicament, and came back to the same all-purpose conclusion – America and Britain were in the grasp of the Jew:

'Never before has there been a war so typically and exclusively Jewish. I have at least compelled them to discard their masks . . . Well, we have lanced the Jewish abscess; and the world of the future will be eternally grateful to us.'

By late April 1945, Hitler had entirely

retreated to his bunker beneath the Berlin Chancellery, hiding in what his architect Speer called 'the Isle of the Departed' – a suffocating concrete labyrinth illuminated by sallow bulbs, which trembled, registering the fact that what little remained of Berlin was being subjected to a ferocious barrage of high-explosive shells as the Russians assailed the ruins of the city.

The inhabitants of the underworld lost track of time; a numb silence prevailed. Hitler's refusal to countenance defeat created an atmosphere of unreality, and secretaries continued to take directives to non-existent armies, execution orders for officers who had failed, and reprimands for those already dead. Violent squabbles occurred. All the staff had appalling migraines, and suffered from acute claustrophobia. Many were sustained only by amphetamines and morphine. The sour air stank of fear and sweat. Everybody wanted to smoke, but Hitler forbade this.

Hitler stayed awake most of the night and slept late. Perched in the corner of an upright sofa in his office, he dictated a stream of memos giving his generals instructions on how to win the war, whilst simultaneously blaming them for Germany's defeat. He spent much of his time toying with a favourite golden labrador puppy. His hair was lank and his eyes dull; spittle dribbled from the corners of his mouth. His left hand developed a tremor, as did his left leg; he controlled this by wrapping it tightly round the leg of a chair or sofa, tensing furiously. His diet consisted principally of cake and vegetable soup.

He showed no concern for the fate of his people; he took no responsibility for the defeat. He thought only of himself. He ordered a scorched-earth policy, and the destruction of anything which might be used to rebuild Germany after the war:

'If the war is lost, the people will be lost also', he noted. 'In any case, only those who are inferior will remain after this struggle . . .' By 26 April 1945 the Red Army was a mile from the bunker. The Reich was in chaos. Himmler and Goering both attempted to do deals with the Allies, to avoid capitulation to the Soviet Union; the army rushed west to surrender to the British and Americans.

On the evening of 29 April, with the enemy only streets away, Hitler married Eva Braun. They drank champagne, and talked about the old days. Hitler, armed with cake, retired to dictate his Last Political Will and Testament. In this he stated: 'I myself, as founder and creator of the movement, have preferred death to cowardly abdication or even capitulation.'

On the afternoon of 30 April, Hitler and Eva Braun shut themselves in his room. She took poison. He shot himself. Hitler's chauffeur burned their bodies in the garden, using 200 litres of petrol. With Hitler's death, an evil spell was lifted. Everybody in the bunker lit cigarettes; a few days later, Germany surrendered. The war had cost the lives of 50 million.

LIFE AND TIMES

Julius Caesar
Hitler
Monet
Van Gogh
Beethoven
Mozart
Mother Teresa
Florence Nightingale
Anne Frank
Napoleon

LIFE AND TIMES

JFK
Martin Luther King
Marco Polo
Christopher Columbus
Stalin
William Shakespeare
Oscar Wilde
Castro
Gandhi
Einstein

FURTHER MINI SERIES
INCLUDE

THEY DIED TOO YOUNG

Elvis
James Dean
Buddy Holly
Jimi Hendrix
Sid Vicious
Marc Bolan
Ayrton Senna
Marilyn Monroe
Jim Morrison

THEY DIED TOO YOUNG

Malcolm X
Kurt Cobain
River Phoenix
John Lennon
Glenn Miller
Isadora Duncan
Rudolph Valentino
Freddie Mercury
Bob Marley

FURTHER MINI SERIES
INCLUDE

ILLUSTRATED POETS

Robert Burns
Shakespeare
Oscar Wilde
Emily Dickinson
Christina Rossetti
Shakespeare's Love Sonnets